Whispers & Wonders

Vandana Rao

BookLeaf Publishing

India | USA | UK

Presentation by *BookLeaf Publishing*

Web: www.bookleafpub.com

E-mail: info@bookleafpub.com

ISBN: 9789363317932

First edition 2024

ACKNOWLEDGEMENT

This book would not have been possible without the unwavering support and love of my incredible family.

To my parents, brother and sis-in-law(more like my sister) who have been my constant pillars of strength. Your endless encouragement, wisdom and belief in me has been the foundation upon which I've built my dreams. Thank you for always being there, guiding me with your boundless love and patience.

To my Aaradhya a.k.a Aaru & Ayaan – you both are the light of my life and my greatest inspiration, your infectious enthusiasm and unyielding love have unearthed my passion for writing which was in deep slumber. Thank you for the countless moments you've spent cheering me on and reminding me to find joy in every little thing. This book is as much yours as it is mine.

Tribes of 40 and beyond(an FB page) – Thank you for reading my stories and poems. Grateful to each and every single one of you who have pushed me to do this and I will be forever grateful. Forever indebted for the life long connections I have made here. You all have my heart ♥

To all the poets and storytellers who have inspired me over the years, thank you for your incredible work. You have sparked my imagination and are the real OG's.

Lastly, but definitely not the least, folks at Bookleaf Publishing! You have made my dreams come true. Forever Indebted.

PREFACE

Hello there! Welcome to my book of poems and stories. It's my first-time writing, and I'm excited to share these with you. Inside, you'll find poems pieces that I've written with lots of heart and a bit of fun.

These pages are like windows to my imagination. Some poems might make you laugh, some might make you think, and others might take you on unexpected adventures. I hope these words bring you joy and maybe, a little bit of magic.

So, make yourself comfortable, grab a drink, and let's dive into this journey together. I hope you enjoy reading as much as I enjoyed writing!

Happy reading!

Magic

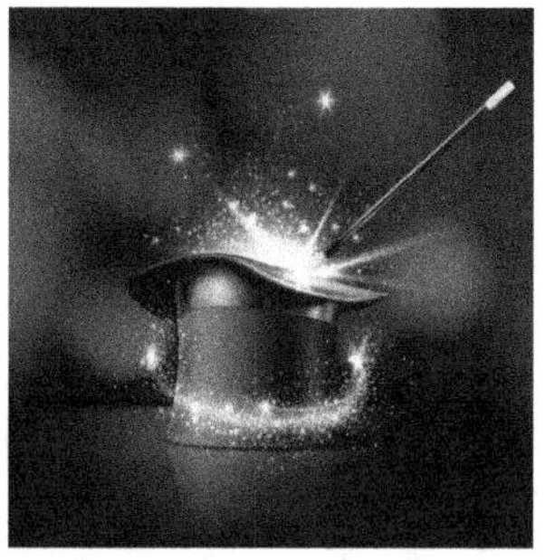

I remember the first poem I read,
simple words strung together,
a small, quiet magic,
like a whisper in the still night.

No grand rhymes or elaborate patterns,
just honest thoughts,
felt deeply and shared plainly,
like a friend's gentle advice.

It spoke of small moments,
a sunrise over the horizon,
the scent of fresh rain on dusty streets,
the feeling of holding hands in silence.

It showed how beauty could be found
in everyday things,
in the way light filters through trees,
in the soft laughter of loved ones.

This poem opened a door,
to a world where words could capture
the essence of feelings,
making the ordinary into extraordinary.

It made me see poetry
not as something lofty or distant,
but as a way to hold close
the simple, tender truths of life.

The Wind

The wind whispers through the trees,
Softly calling my name,
I stand alone, feeling its gentle touch,
Embracing the serenity it brings.

The leaves dance in rhythm,
A symphony orchestrated by nature,
The sky blushes pink,
As day transitions into night.

In the solitude of nature,
I find solace in every breeze,
Whispering stories of distant lands,
And the secrets they keep.

As night falls, the wind grows softer,
A lullaby of the earth,
Singing me to sleep under the stars,
Each gust a tender reminder of nature's grace.

The branches sway in unison,
Their shadows casting delicate patterns,
A reminder that even in the quiet,
There is a melody to be found,
Written by nature's own hands.

Cup of bliss

The aroma of coffee fills the morning air,
a rich, deep scent that wakes me gently.
Warmth cradles my hands, a quiet promise of
peace.
Each sip a soft embrace,
like a familiar, comforting touch.

Steam curls upward,
dancing in the light of dawn.
The world outside is still,
but inside, there's a gentle hum of contentment.
The bitterness and warmth blend,
a small ritual that starts the day.

But when shared with someone special,
the whole experience transforms.
Their laughter mingles with the steam,
a melody that makes the moment heavenly.
The simple act of sipping side by side,
turns into a sacred dance of connection.

Conversations flow, soft and warm,
as the coffee deepens the bond.
In their presence,
the ritual becomes a cherished embrace,
a shared warmth that turns an ordinary morning
into something profoundly beautiful.

Sunset

As the sun dips below the horizon,
The sky paints a masterpiece,
Reds and oranges blend,
Creating a vibrant maze.

I sit quietly, absorbing the beauty,
The day turning into night,
The silence is profound,
Nature's way of bidding farewell to the day.

The beauty of the sunset,
Mirrors the transient moments,
A serenade of colors,
An ode to nature's splendor.

The colors deepen, spreading across the sky,
Each hue a reflection of the earth's passion,
Twilight a canvas,
Of memories painted by the sun's descent.

As the horizon swallows the last light,
The world is cloaked in twilight,
A gentle reminder that endings,
Are but preludes to new beginnings,
In the ever-turning wheel of nature's time.

A Wish

The next time you fall in love, I hope it ignites a fire in your soul—lighting up your life with undeniable brilliance.

*May this love be so deep
and true that it heals every scar and banishes every fear, enveloping you in unending bliss.*

Finding someone who desires you is easy, but discovering a soul with pure intentions and unwavering love is a rare gift.

*Someone whose every touch and word are filled with
passion and tenderness, who finds endless delight in your presence and never tires of adoring you.*

*They will see your worth, especially
on days when you find it hardest to love yourself.*

*May you find that extraordinary soul who fears
nothing more than losing someone as wondrous
as you.*

*And most importantly, may you find a
love that chooses you, fiercely and
unapologetically, every single day.
You are a beacon of love and light, deserving of
the deepest and most passionate love.*

*Always remember that you are perfect just as
you are,
worthy of all the love and happiness the world
has to offer.
You are not hard to love; you are a
miracle to be loved and cherished.*

*Never doubt your worth or your capacity to
inspire profound
love in others.
You are enough, just the way you are.*

Moonlight Wonder

The moonlight bathes the meadow,
Turning it into a magical place,
Where dreams take flight,
And the heart finds peace.

I walk under the stars,
Each step a journey into the night,
The laughter of the crickets,
Echoing in the stillness.

The night holds me close,
In a tender embrace,
Whispering secrets of the earth,
In the language of the moonlight.

The gentle glow of the moon,
Illuminates the landscape,
Highlighting the beauty of nature,
A mirror of the world's quiet grace.

I find a spot to rest,
Lying on the soft grass,
The world around me fades,
Leaving only the moon's gentle light.

In this meadow of dreams,
Time stands still,
And I lose myself,
In the serene beauty of the night.

The stars above, countless and brilliant,
Weave a sight of wonder,
Their light a guide through the dark,
A testament to the enduring beauty,
Of the beautiful world.

Loving you

You are the melody that sets my heart aflame, a symphony of desire that ignites my every sense. You are the verse that dances upon my lips, a cascade of words that stir the depths of my being with a passionate allure.

You are the confidant of my soul, sharing the laughter of our joyous moments and the intimacy of our deepest conversations, each instant spent together a timeless embrace of affection.

You are the other half of my soul, our connection a celestial bond that transcends mere mortal existence, intertwining our spirits in a dance of cosmic destiny.

You are the embodiment of passion, our love a tempest of fervor that consumes us in a whirlwind of ecstasy, every touch, every kiss an ode to the sublime unity of our hearts.

You are my sanctuary, in your arms I find solace, acceptance, and the profound sense of belonging that makes every moment with you feel like coming home.

*You are my amor, mi amor, and no measure of
time could ever contain the depth of my
affection for you, for my love for you knows no
bounds.*

Moonlight whispers

In the moonlight, your face shines bright,
A smile that fills me with sheer delight.
Tonight, I just want to hold you tight,
Feel your touch, making everything right.

In my chest, a fire starts to grow,
With every secret shared, our bond does glow.
Captivated by you, in the moon's soft glow,
Your scent, like a sweet breeze, to and fro.

Your hair, like waves upon the shore,
Your smile, a light I adore.
In dreams, you're near, I can't ask for more,
With you, doubts and fears no longer soar.

Your voice, a melody, pure and clear,
Even from afar, it's you I hold dear.
At dawn, when stars disappear,
In dreams, our love story becomes clear.

In the quiet of night, our souls align,
No shadows cast, no doubts malign.
No ghosts to haunt, our love does shine,
In memories cherished, our hearts divine.

So let me hold you close, my dear,
In this moment, let our fears disappear.
In your arms, doubts find their end,
In your love, my heart will always mend.

Journey

In the soft glow of dawn's early light,
Parents embark on a journey, love burning
bright.
Through diapers and giggles, the first steps we
take,
They guide us with love, each new memory to
make.

Childhood days, filled with laughter and play,
In their arms, we find comfort each day.
They teach us to walk, they teach us to speak,
A foundation of love that's strong, not weak.

In their embrace, we learn kindness and grace,
The warmth of their love, a comforting space.
They instill in us values, compassion, and care,
Lessons we carry with us, everywhere.

As school days unfold, with lessons to learn,
They are there, for support, our hearts they earn.
They celebrate victories, console in defeat,

Their love, a constant, so pure and sweet.

Teenage years, a rollercoaster of emotion,
They navigate with love and devotion.
Through rebellions and dreams taking flight,
They stand by us, a beacon in the night.

In adulthood's journey, they continue to guide,
Through weddings and careers, by our side.
Their love deepens, evolving and true,
A bond unbreakable, a love that grew.

Then comes a stage, where roles reverse,
As time takes its toll, and health may disperse.
Yet in their eyes, a timeless love remains,
A connection unbroken, despite life's strains.

In their wisdom, lessons of resilience we find,
Unconditional love, a treasure so kind.
Through joy and sorrow, the trials we face,
Their love teaches us strength and grace.

As the sun sets, and shadows grow long,
They become memories, a cherished song.
Their love endures, like a timeless rhyme,
A melody echoing through the sands of time.

And what we learn from them, a precious trove,
Unconditional love, the foundation of love.

Rain-Kissed Moments

The rain falls gently,
Each drop a kiss from the heavens,
Reminding me of the earth's vitality,
And the freshness it brings.

I stand alone,
Under the shelter of trees,
As the world fades away,
Leaving only the symphony of rain.

The rain sings a song,
Of nature's rejuvenation,
Each drop a testament,
To the cycle of life.

I dance in the rain,
Lost in its gentle embrace,
The rhythm of the falling water,
A backdrop to the earth's melody.

The scent of wet earth rises,
A fragrance of renewal and life,
The raindrops, tiny musicians,
Playing a harmonious tune,
On leaves, stones, and streams.

The world becomes a watercolor painting,
With every droplet adding a new hue,
A masterpiece in the making,
Crafted by the patient hand of nature,
In the language of rain.

Forest of Hearts

In the heart of the forest,
Where the world is a whisper,
I find peace waiting,
A beacon of tranquility.

The trees stand tall,
Guardians of ancient secrets,
Their leaves rustling,
In a symphony of life.

I wander through the forest,
Lost in nature's beauty,
Every step a journey,
Into the depths of the earth.

The scent of pine and earth,
A heady mix of nature's essence,
Reminds me of the purity,
Of the world around me.

I pause to listen to the songbirds,
Their melodies weaving through the trees,
A chorus of nature's finest,
Celebrating the richness of the forest.

The forest floor, a giver of life,
Moss and fern in soft green hues,
A carpet laid by nature's hand,
Inviting exploration,
And a deeper connection to the earth.

Friendly Shenanigans

To my friend who holds my hand
and stands right by my side,
who cheers me up
and fills me with pride.

You make me feel like I'm standing tall (even
though I am short)
and whole, not broken at all.
You always listen
to whatever I say (even if it's gibberish)
and make me laugh
every single day.

You're my snack buddy, my partner in crime
(yeah, you heard that right)
turning every moment into pure delight.
You sit with me quietly,
knowing it's enough,
and help me through
when days get tough.

We dance like crazy,
and laugh till we drop,
with you, the fun just won't stop.
I'm so lucky to call you my best friend,
and grateful for you, from beginning to end.

Rediscover

I've always been here, lovingly beside you,
Through every rise and fall we've faced.
Why did you lose sight of our passion?
When did everything veer off course?

I know you're lost and longing,
Feeling as though you don't belong.
I saw this coming, we must stay strong,
But finding me now might be too long.

Let me guide you back,
To rediscover our shared flame.
But you must seek your own path,
Even if it seems distant and tame.

We need to connect deeply,
In the depths of your beating heart.
Only then can we ignite anew,
And make a fresh, passionate start.

Listen closely to our love's melody,
Ignore the discord and strife.
Your fears and doubts will try to deceive,
But our bond will guide your life.

They've held you captive too long,
Kept you from our true embrace.
But together we can break free,
If you choose to seek our place.

Don't let them pull you down,
Into their world of deceit.
They may pretend to be you,
But our love cannot be beat.

Trust me, you deserve more,
Than what they try to steal.
Let our passion reclaim your life,
And show you what's truly real.

Symphony of passion

In the hush before dawn,
I ache for you,
longing to feel your warmth beside me,
to whisper secrets only we know.

In that place between sleep and waking,
I yearn for your touch,
a gentle caress that awakens my senses,
sending shivers down my spine.

In the calm of early morning,
I embrace the day with you,
finding solace in your presence,
knowing we face the world together.

In my heart,
I am wrapped in your love,
a blanket of comfort and joy,
shielding me from life's uncertainties.

In the air around us,
I breathe in the scent of your skin,
intoxicating and familiar,
a reminder of our intimate bond.

In your eyes,
I see the fire of your desire,
burning bright with longing,
reflecting the depth of our connection.

In every caress,
I rediscover our love,
each touch a testament to passion,
a dance of hearts beating as one.

Deep within me,
I burn for you,
my soul ignited,
forever yearning for our eternal embrace.

Serenade of the heart

In the realm where love and romance merge,
I believe in chances divine;
Believe in the magic of true romance,
Where hearts dance in a passionate trance.

I believe fate gives us a guiding hand,
Leading us to where dreams expand.
In the soft whisper of the evening breeze,
Love blossoms under moonlit trees.

I still hold faith in the goodness of hearts,
In kindness that sets love apart;
Believe in dreams that soar and fly,
In love's embrace, where souls unify.

When life's journey takes a rugged road,
Love paves a path where dreams unfold.
Life's rhythm flows, not bound by time,
Each ending a prelude to love's prime.

You're captivated by this romantic tune,
Feeling each verse beneath the moon.
Eager to discover what fate will bestow,
In love's story, where hearts glow.

Tomorrow holds promises yet untold,
In each line, love's tale will unfold.

Memories

*Inhaling deeply, memories of you flood my
mind,
Guiding me to seek rainbows high, cuddle pets,
and chase butterflies kind.*

*The ocean's roar, sands and pebbles, flowers
kissed by the sun's embrace,
Days of warm rain, nights humid and hot,
winter's dawn with sunlight's grace.*

*Antique treasures, clocks that tick, art both
modern and old,
Early mornings waking, our favorite song,
stories yet untold.*

*These cherished things, they soothe my soul and
draw you near,
As I bow my head, breathe deeply, holding back
a tear.*

*Yet amidst these clouds, echoes of regret still
dance,
Like dancers once beloved, in a memory's
trance.
I'm adrift in this sea, surrendering to the waves,
Your words now soft lullabies, soothing me in
gentle caves.*

*So I breathe in your essence, forever and
evermore,
A fragrance that lingers, keeping you close, as
before.*

Reflections

In a small house by the sea, an old woman lives,
happy and free.
Her hair's all gray, eyes still bright, sitting by
the window, bathed in light.

Her hands are wrinkled, steps real slow, but her
heart's young, with a warm glow.
She thinks back to when she was younger,
dreaming in dreams, believing it all.

Fields of green flash in her mind, a girl with
hopes, one of a kind.
Worked so hard, gave it her best, built her life,
passed every test.

She recalls love and friends so dear, laughing
and talking, voices clear.
Faced with tough times, some nights so long, but
always stayed brave, always strong.

*Her kids grew up, love spread wide, in their
smiles, she found her pride.
Taught them kindness, showed the way, watched
them grow, day by day.*

*Now she's old, but there's no fear, knows she
lived her life sincere.
With a gentle sigh, a smile shows, she lived a
good life, and it shows.*

Midnight longing

*In the deep of night, my love, when silence
wraps around, and the hour grows late, my
mind, heart, and soul reach for you; aching,
yearning, craving the warmth of your unique
energy*

*I long to breathe your scent, feel your strength
enfolding, cheek against your chest, lost in the
rhythm of your heartbeat; fragile strength
cradled, as I once gave mine to you, long ago.*

*When your chin grazes my head, your chest rises
and falls beneath my touch, breath warming my
cheek, moments before our lips meet, only then,
home is found anew.*

*For in these quiet hours, thoughts of you flood
my being, weaving memories with dreams, where
time*

loses its grip and distance fades to nothing.

Your presence lingers in the shadows, echoes in every whisper of the night, beckoning me closer, to the place where souls meet, and love's embrace knows no bounds.

So, I wait, in the stillness of the night, heart open, longing, for the moment you return, and our worlds collide once more, in the timeless dance of love.

Winter's Beauty

The first snowflakes fall gently,
A silent ballet of nature,
Covering the world in a blanket of white,
A symbol of purity and new beginnings.

I walk through the winter landscape,
Breath visible in the cold air,
Each step a testament to the season,
Strengthened by the quiet beauty.

The trees stand bare and silent,
Their branches adorned with snow,
A scene of tranquil beauty,
Reflecting the quiet strength of winter.

I find a cozy spot by the fire,
The warmth contrasting with the icy world
outside,
Nature's duality a comforting balm,
Against the winter's bite.

The crunch of snow underfoot,
A symphony of winter's touch,
Each flake a unique masterpiece,
Created by the hands of the cold.

The quiet of the winter night,
Holds a promise of stillness,
A time to reflect and find peace,
In the serene embrace of winter,
Where the world sleeps in quiet wonder.

Raindrops & Reverie

In your eyes, I find my universe,
A spark that sets my heart ablaze.
We sit by the window, rain dancing outside,
Your laughter is my favorite melody.

Every touch of your hand,
A promise of forever.
We lose ourselves in conversation,
Sharing dreams and fears,
Every word a bond,
Every glance a silent vow.

Your lips, a soft caress,
Speak of love without words.
We dream of distant places,
Where our hearts can roam free.

Each shared look, a promise,
Each whispered secret, a treasure.

In your embrace, I am whole,
In your gaze, I see eternity.

The rain outside mirrors our passion,
Each drop a testament to our love.
We plan futures, build castles in the sky,
Imagining a life where our souls unite.

Your love, a guiding star,
Leads me through the darkest night.
Together, we conquer the world,
Bound by a love that knows no end.

Children of the sun

Their beauty was like the morning sun,
Bright and warm, touching everyone.
With laughter like the gentle breeze,
They danced through fields with endless ease.

They ran through the fields of hope,
Not knowing what they sought.
But they knew when they found it,
It would be all they ever wanted.

With each step, their hearts grew lighter,
As if the world was getting brighter.
Hand in hand, they faced the sun,
Believing their journey had just begun.

The sky brightened their darkness,
And they saw it on the slope.
It was coming straight toward them,
And they knew they'd found their hope.

In the distance, a rainbow glowed,
A bridge to dreams they now rode.
Their eyes sparkled with delight,
As day turned into a magical night.

And as the stars lit up the sky,
They felt a peace they couldn't deny.
With hope in hand and love all around,
In the fields of dreams, they were forever bound.

Breathless Love

Our breaths mix in the night air,
The city sleeps, but we are wide awake,
Lost in the wonder of each other.
Our fingers trace invisible lines,
Mapping the contours of our love.

Your touch ignites my soul,
A fire that burns brighter with each kiss.
In the darkness, we find light,
In each other, we find home.

Your scent lingers in the air,
A memory that never fades.
We talk about everything and nothing,
Every word a caress, every laugh a kiss.

Our bodies close,
Lost in the rhythm of our hearts.
In your arms, I feel complete,
In your touch, I find my strength.

The city lights create a halo around us,
A cocoon of intimacy and passion.
We explore each other, discovering new depths,
Every moment a new chapter in our love story.

Your eyes, a mirror to your soul,
Reflect the love you hold for me.
Together, we weave a narrative of us,
A love that feels both timeless and eternal.

Home

A house is made of brick and stone,
But a home is where love has grown.
Children run with joy and glee,
Filling rooms with laughter, free.

In the kitchen, meal's prepared,
With love and care, it's all shared.
Dreams are woven in each room,
Turning walls from gray to bloom.

Elders bless with wisdom's light,
Guiding paths both day and night.
Love fills corners, warm and bright,
Turning shadows into light.

Whispers shared in the evening calm,
Hands held close, a soothing balm.
Memories crafted every day,
In love's embrace, hearts always stay.

Windows open to the sun,
Showing days of joy begun.
Love's the thread that binds it tight,
Turning houses into homes, just right.

Moonlit dreams

Beneath the moon's soft, silver light,
She stands alone in the quiet night.
Her heart whispers a silent tune,
Of dreams and hopes under the moon.

Her eyes trace shadows on its face,
Wishing for his warm embrace.
In the stillness, thoughts take flight,
A longing deep, a hidden light.

She craves the touch of his gentle hand,
A love that's more than she can stand.
Her passion burns, a steady flame,
As she softly whispers his name.

Memories of their first sweet kiss,
In the moonlight's gentle bliss.
The way he held her close and tight,
Underneath the starry night.

Though miles stretch between them now,
Love will find a way somehow.
In the moon's embrace, she dreams,
Of love that's truer than it seems.

Her thoughts are like the ocean's tide,
Flowing with a love she cannot hide.
A passion that the moon ignites,
In the depth of silent nights.

In the moon's glow, she sees his face,
Her heart beats in a timeless space.
She knows that love will find its way,
Through night to dawn, and into day.

So she stands beneath the moon's bright beam,
Lost in love's enduring dream.
Her soul wrapped in the night's romance,
In moonlight's tender, endless dance.

The End of Us

I thought you were the one for me
Until you showed me why we can't be.
I trusted you'd care for my heart,
But you hurt me, tore me apart.

I thought you'd love me right,
Knowing my past, my endless fight.
But you hurt me like the rest,
Left me with pain, feeling stressed.

Bit by bit, you broke my heart,
Leaving me to wonder why we part.
I decided it was time to leave,
Not because I don't believe,

But because I'm tired of asking you,
To love me right, to see me through.
I'm tired of feeling all alone,
In your arms, a heart of stone.

I know now you're not the one,
You didn't care when I was done.
You smiled when I said goodbye,
No sadness, no tears in your eye.

Maybe you waited for me to leave,
For the day I'd cease to grieve.
And maybe, you waited too long,
For me to see where I belong.

Midnight Dance

The warmth of your skin,
A reminder of everything beautiful.
We dance in the living room,
Bare feet on cold tiles,

Music plays softly,
But our hearts beat louder.
Every spin, a declaration of love,
Every touch, a promise of eternity.

In your arms, I find my rhythm,
In your eyes, my forever.
We move in perfect harmony,
Our bodies speaking a language of their own.

Your smile, a beacon of joy,
Guides me through the dance of life.
We sway to the music, lost in each other,
Every step a testament to our love.

The world outside ceases to exist,
In this moment, only we remain.
The music changes, but our love remains
constant,
A melody that never fades.

We dance through the night,
Every movement a celebration of us.
Your touch sends shivers down my spine,
A reminder of the passion we share.

In your embrace, I find my solace,
In your love, my sanctuary belongs.

Journey to myself

*I've spent my life trying to find
Who I am, what I want, where I belong.
People told me what I should be,
Tried to fit me into their box.*

*Everyone had opinions of who I should be,
Why I should be like them.
But their ideas never made me happy,
Never felt like the real me.*

*To find the hardest answers,
I stepped out of my comfort zone,
Looked deep into my soul,
Listened to my own heart.*

*Turns out, I already had the answers,
Hidden deep inside.
The world tries to shape you,
But it's not about who you should be.*

I'm tired of labels,
Won't follow anyone else's path.
Only I know what makes me happy,
What I want in life.

I want what everyone wants, but more
More than happiness, I want to feel alive.
More than comfort, I want to grow,
To be the best I can be.

My heart's been hurt, but still beats strong,
I learned from failures, matured and got better.
Never stayed down, always looked to the sun.
I'm unique, special, beautiful in my own way.

Most of all, I'll always be myself,
Broken, beautiful, finding my way.
If you want to find me, look to the horizon,
Chasing dreams, reaching for the stars.

I've got one chance at this life,
And I'll always give it my all.

Fireside Embrace

Your smile, a sunrise after a long night,
Fills my world with color.
We sit by the fire,
Hands close,
Lost in each other,
The world outside fades away.

Every flicker of the flame,
A reflection of our passion,
Every whisper of the wind,
A testament to our bond.

In your warmth, I find solace,
In your love, I find home.
The fire crackles, casting shadows on the wall,
Creating a dance of light and dark.

We talk about our dreams, our hopes,
Building a future together.
Your love, a beacon of light,
Guides me through the darkest times.

With you, I am invincible,
Together, we can conquer the world.
The night grows colder, but our love burns
brighter,
A flame that never dies.

We hold each other close,
Finding comfort in our embrace.
Every kiss, a promise of forever,
Every touch, a declaration of love.

In your arms, I find my strength,
And in your heart, my forever home.

Sunset memories

On the beach, where the sky meets the sea,
She sits alone, lost in memory.
The sun sets, painting the sky so bright,
In colors that fade into the night.

Each wave gently kisses the sand,
She holds onto memories, hand in hand.
They walked and talked along this shore,
Their love's dance, forevermore.

They laughed and dreamed beneath the sun,
Two hearts together, becoming one.
But time moves on, things rearrange,
Leaving memories in its range.

Now she sits in the soft twilight,
Where their love once shone so bright.
Her heart still feels his gentle touch,
A love that meant so much, so much.

In the whispers of the ocean's song,
She feels him near, though he is gone.
The salty breeze, a warm embrace,
Brings back memories of his face.

Her thoughts drift to their special place,
Where they shared dreams and found grace.
The stars above, they seem to know,
Their love's depth in ebb and flow.

She smiles through tears, a mix so true,
Of love remembered, still so new.
For in her heart, his love resides,
In every wave that softly glides.

As night falls and stars align,
Their love was pure, a lasting sign.
Though they said goodbye, love's bond won't
die,
In every sunset, his love will fly.

So on this beach where memories roam,
She finds solace in their love's sweet home.
Love transcends time, forever true,
In every sunset, his love shines through.

Coffee Moments

In your arms, I find peace,
A quiet place in a noisy world.

We share a cup of coffee,
Our fingers touch,
A simple act,
Yet it sets my heart racing.
The aroma of coffee mingles with the scent of
you,
Creating a perfect blend of comfort and love.

Every sip, a shared moment,
Every glance, a silent promise.
In your presence, I find my calm,
In your love, my sanctuary.

The morning light filters through the curtains,
Casting a golden glow on your face.
We sit in silence, content in each other's
company,
Finding joy in the little things.

Your laughter, a sound I cherish,
Your touch, a comfort I seek.
Together, we create a world of our own,
A sanctuary of love and peace.

Every moment with you is a treasure,
A memory I hold dear.
We talk about our dreams, our fears,
Building a life together.

Your love, a guiding star,
Leads me through the darkest night.
With you, I am complete,
And together, we find our forever.

Worthy Love

I hope you find a love so true,
With no mixed signals, just me and you.
Across the room, our eyes will meet,
A smile that makes our joy complete.

I hope you find a love that's strong,
Who meets you halfway, where you belong.
Faithful, steady, always there,
A bond that no one else can tear.

I hope you find a love that forgives,
Sees your flaws, yet still believes.
Through mistakes, they'll help you grow,
Irreplaceable, even in woe.

I hope you find a love that cheers,
Supports your dreams, calms your fears.
In your corner, day by day,
Choosing you in every way.

I hope you find a love that's sweet,
Grateful for each little feat.
Still impressed with what you do,
Truly values the real you.

I hope you find your closest friend,
Laughter and joy that never end.
Your loudest laugh, your biggest smile,
Your number one fan through every mile.

Remember it's your fate,
The right love is worth the wait.
For you deserve a love so great,
A love that's perfect, never late.

Walk on the beach

Your voice, a soothing balm,
Calms the storm within me.
We walk under the moonlight,
Barefoot on the beach,
Sharing secrets, and dreaming dreams.

The ocean sings a song just for us,
And we dance to its rhythm,
Two hearts beating as one.
Every wave, a reminder of our endless love,
Every step, a journey we take together.

The moonlight casts a glow on your face,
Highlighting the beauty I adore.
We talk about our pasts, our futures,
Creating memories.

Your laughter, a melody I cherish,
Your touch, a promise of forever.
Together, we build a dream,
A life filled with love and passion.

The sand beneath our feet is cool,
But the embrace of your love keeps me warm.
We walk for hours, lost in each other,
The world around us fading away.

In your eyes, I see our future,
A vision of love and happiness.
With you, every step is an adventure,
And every night an endless journey.

Gift of age

Age is a gift I now see,
For the first time, I'm just being me.
Not my body, I sometimes frown,
At wrinkles and sags, looking down.

But I wouldn't trade my friends so dear,
My joyful life, my family near.
With gray hair and a rounder face,
I've found wisdom and love in this place.

Friends gone too soon showed me the way,
To cherish the freedom in each day.
I read through the night, sleep until noon,
And dance alone under the moon.

Sometimes forgetful, but that's okay,
Important things still find their way.
A broken heart heals, making me strong,
Laughing through life, where I belong.

Blessed with silver hair and lines,
Each one a memory that shines.
Many didn't get this chance,
To laugh, to love, to dance.

I say "no" and "yes" with ease,
Aging with grace, doing as I please.
I like being old, I've come to see,
The freedom to be truly me.

I won't live forever, but while I stay,
I'll enjoy each moment, come what may.
And every day, with joy so sweet,
I'll have dessert, life's final treat.

Safe Haven

You are my safe haven,
My lighthouse in the storm.
We lie on the grass,
Staring at the stars,
And I realize,
You are my everything.

The night sky whispers our secrets,
And every star shines for us.
Your touch, a gentle reminder,
That we are bound by more than love,
By destiny, by fate, by the universe.

The wind rustles the leaves,
Creating a harmony of nature.
We talk about our dreams, our fears,
Finding solace in each other's arms.

Your love, a beacon of light,
Guides me through the darkest times.
With you, I am invincible,
Together, we can conquer the world.

The night grows colder, but our love shines
brighter,
A flame that never dies.

We hold each other close,
Finding comfort in our embrace.

Every kiss, a promise of forever,
Every touch, a declaration of love.
In your arms, I find my strength,
And with you, I face any storm.

Unwavering love

If a man truly loves you,
He will move mountains and skies,
Just to be by your side,
Where his true love resides.

He will listen with care,
Feelings he'll never dismiss,
He'll work hard every day,
To bring laughter and bliss.

He will guard your heart gently,
Never cause you pain,
And if he ever stumbles,
He'll apologize again.

He'll speak with kind words,
Never shout or show scorn,
With deep love and respect,
Your heart he'll adorn.

He'll say you're his world,
And give you his all,
For a love so divine,
So pure and so tall.

He humbles himself,
Wants to be your peace,
Your provider, protector,
Where calmness will cease.

For he knows you are sacred,
Sent from above,
And he'll treat you with grace,
In a life filled with love.

Culinary Romance

Your laughter is the sweetest sound,
A melody that brings joy to my soul.

We cook together,
Our hands brush,
And in that simple moment,
I find a thousand reasons to love you.

The kitchen fills with the aroma of our love,
Every dish a testament to our shared life.
Your smile, a sprinkle of joy,
Your touch, a dash of passion.

Together, we create a feast of love,
A banquet of dreams and desires.
The clinking of utensils,
A harmony of our love.

We move in perfect rhythm,
Creating a masterpiece of flavors.

Your touch, a gentle reminder,
Of the passion we share.

We share a meal, a moment, a memory,
Finding joy in the simple things.
Your love, a guiding star,
Leads me through the darkest night.

With you, I am complete,
And every meal becomes a celebration of us.

Glances of Eternity

The way you look at me,
As if I'm the only person in the world,
Makes my heart skip a beat.

We share a quiet evening,
Talk about everything and nothing,
And in your presence, I am complete.

Every word, a stroke of love,
Every glance, a painting of passion.
In the silence, our souls speak,
In the stillness, our hearts beat as one.

You are my muse, my lover, my friend,
In your love, I find my end and beginning.
The fire crackles, casting shadows on the wall,
Creating a dance of light and dark.

We talk about our dreams and our future,
Finding joy in the simple moments.
Every glance you give me is a promise,
Every touch a whisper of forever.

In the quiet of the evening,
We find our voices,
Every sigh a shared secret,
Every laugh a testament to our bond.

You are my endless horizon,
And together, we traverse the landscapes of love.
With you, every second is a cherished memory,
Every day a new adventure in our shared
journey.

Carousel adventures

In the park with tall rides and twinkling lights,
Mommy and daughter, hand in hand,
Step through the gates into wonderland.

Carousel horses, up and down,
Giggles, smiles, all around,
Ferris wheel reaching for the sky,
Up they go, with a joyful sigh.

Cotton candy, fluffy and pink,
Sweetness shared, no need to think,
Popcorn popped, buttery smell,
Happy tummies, they could tell.

Roller coaster, wild and fast,
Screams of joy, a thrilling blast,
Kids laughter, loud and clear,
Mommy's heart, filled with cheer.

Shooting hoops, winning rings,
Stuffed toy prizes, such joyful things,
Bumper cars with bumps and cheers,
She's wiping away happy tears.

Spinning tea cups, dizzy fun,
Twirling 'round 'til they were done,
Lights dimmed, stars began to gleam,
Time to leave, but hearts still beam.

Dreaming of their special day,
In the park, where they did play,
Mommy and daughter, their love so true,
A day of fun, just them two.

Urban Romance

Every moment with you,
Is a memory I cherish.

We explore the city,
Hand in hand,
And in every adventure,
I fall in love with you all over again.

The streets tell our story,
Every corner, a chapter of passion,
Every step, a verse of romance.

In the hustle of the city, we find our calm,
In the chaos, our peace.
Your love is my journey,
Your heart, my destination.

We discover hidden gems,
Secret spots only we know.
Each place holds a memory,
A moment frozen in time.

Your laughter echoes in the alleys,
Your smile lights up the darkest streets.
Together, we conquer the city,
Two hearts beating as one.

As the night falls,
We find new places,
Every street and café, a canvas for our love.

Every moment is a celebration,
Every adventure a testament to our bond.
In each other, we find the world,
And every journey becomes a shared dream.

With you, every day is an exploration,
Every second a treasure, a promise of our
enduring love.

Beautiful world

A beautiful world would be
where everyone is kind
where smiles are free
and hearts are open

A place where laughter is heard
and children play without fear
where friends gather often
and no one is lonely

Imagine walking by the Great Wall
feeling the history in every stone
or standing before the Taj Mahal
where love is written on marble

Gazing at the Pyramids of Egypt
wonders of time and human will
or wandering through Machu Picchu
where ancient whispers fill the air

Seeing the Northern Lights dance
painting the sky with colors
or diving into the Great Barrier Reef
a world of life under the sea

In this world, dreams come true
and every day is bright
it's a place full of hope and joy
a world we all wish to see

Where wonders both old and new
fill our hearts with awe
and every corner of the earth
feels like a place to call home

Lazy mornings

Sunlight streams through the window
Birds sing softly, welcoming the day
A gentle breeze whispers through the leaves
Curtains dance with the morning light

The air is cool, calm, peaceful
Chai brews, its scent fills the room
No rush, no plans—just stillness
A book waits, pages ready to be turned

Stretch, yawn, sink back into the pillows
Time flows slowly, almost stopping
Every moment savored, unhurried
A lazy morning, simple and serene

Children's giggles, stories told
Hands held, warmth spreads

Together, we make memories
In the softness of this morning

Blankets on the couch, movies play
Whispers of love, gentle and true
No hurry, no haste, just this
A lazy morning, filled with love

Laughter echoes through the rooms
Hearts light, souls content
In these moments, we find our joy
A lazy morning, a family's embrace

Quiet midnight

In the hush of the night
the world asleep, dreams unfolding
I lie awake, heart open
thinking of you

In this midnight hour
I feel your presence
a gentle breeze through the window
brushing my skin like your touch

I remember the way
your fingers traced my face
like a painter, careful and tender
each touch a masterpiece

Our late-night whispers
beneath a canopy of stars
your breath mingling with mine
each word a soft caress

As dawn approaches
the sky slowly brightens
I hold on to this feeling
this quiet longing

Until we meet again
under the same stars
I will keep these midnight musings
tucked away, close to my heart.

Unspoken sparks

In the morning light, she sees him
Eyes soft, smile gentle
Her heart skips a beat, then two
Butterflies dancing in her stomach

When he walks by, her breath catches
She fumbles with her words, her hands
Sweat on her palms, hope in her heart
Does he feel it too?

She doesn't know
That he feels the same way
His heart racing, his mind reeling
Whenever their eyes meet, whenever they speak

Their interactions are electrifying
Each glance a spark, each touch a tease
A brush of fingers, a fleeting touch
Leaving them both breathless, wanting more

He loves her laugh, her spirit
The way she sees the world, the way she cares
He's drawn to her, like a moth to a flame
But he's never found the words

So they dance around their feelings
In stolen moments, in shared smiles
Living in the hope, the possibility
Of love, of togetherness

For now, they hold their feelings close
Cherishing the moments, the stolen glances
Living in the mystery, the anticipation
Of what might and could be

Spring rain

Soft spring rain
falls gently on the earth
awakening flowers
and washing trees clean

Each drop whispers
of new beginnings
of promises made
in the language of nature

Puddles form
reflecting the sky
painted in gray and blue
a changing canvas

The fresh scent of rain
fills the air
a reminder of new life
starting again

Grass drinks deeply
birds sing softly
the world pauses
to breathe in the moment

Soft spring rain
nourishes the earth
brings hope and peace
to a waiting world

In this gentle rain
hope grows
like the first green shoots
in a garden of dreams

Under the eternal stars

Under the stars, we sit in silence,
the night wraps us in its cool embrace,
whispers of the wind play with your hair,
and your eyes, like the stars,
shine with a gentle light.

The world is asleep, but we are awake,
sharing secrets only the night knows.

Your voice, a soothing melody,
weaves stories of tomorrow,
and in your words,
I find hope and courage.

Your laughter mingles with the night,
a soft sound that feels like home,
and in this moment,
time feels like it stops, just for us.

In your arms, I find my peace,
my heart beats in time with yours,
and I know, in this infinite sky,
our love is our guiding star.

Your touch ignites a spark,
a warmth that spreads through me,
our hearts, aflame with love,
under the eternal stars.

I dream of you

In the quiet of the night,
I dream of you,
your eyes, soft and kind,
a smile that brings light to my dark.

In this world of dreams,
there's no rush, no end,
just moments stretched into forever,
where love flows like a gentle stream.

I see your face, clear as dawn,
feel your touch, warm as the sun,
and in this dream,
we are timeless, boundless, whole.

In the garden of my mind,
flowers bloom with your name,
each petal a story,
each fragrance a memory.

When dawn breaks,
I wake with a gentle ache,
your presence lingering like a shadow,
a beautiful ghost in the daylight.

But until the night returns,
I hold onto these dreams,
each one a treasure,
each one a piece of you, of us.

Twilight embrace

As the sun dips low,
the sky blushing softly,
we walk together, hand in hand,
on the cool, smooth sand.

The waves tease us,
with their gentle touch, like your lips,
brushing mine
in fleeting, passionate kisses.

Our laughter mingles with the breeze,
but each kiss we share
speaks louder than words,
a language only we understand.

Footprints behind us,
slowly erased by the sea,
like moments we've lived,
intimately shared,

never truly fading,
but merging into this night.

In this evening's embrace,
under the canopy of stars,
we are two hearts,
surrendering to the magic of now,
where every touch, every glance,
brims with romance and passion,
each moment a cherished eternity.

Silent Connection

When you look at me,
it's like you see something beyond
a spark of light that dances
in the corners of your eyes.

Your gaze is soft,
filled with a sense of warmth
that wraps around my heart,
like a gentle embrace.

In those moments,
I feel a quiet kind of magic,
an unspoken promise
that we're connected in ways
words can't quite capture.

Your eyes hold a love
that seems to understand
every secret I've ever kept,
every dream I've ever whispered.

In your look,
I find the reflection of my soul,
a mirror that holds
all the unspoken truths,
all the quiet hopes.

You look at me
and in your eyes,
I see my own heart
dancing in the light of yours,
forever connected.

Letter to myself!

Dear Younger Me,
In the quiet moments when you doubt yourself,
When the weight of the world seems too heavy,
Remember that you carry a strength within.

Each heartbeat is a whisper of courage,
A testament to your resilience.
In the face of setbacks and fears,
Hold on to your dreams with unwavering faith.

Embrace the journey, with all its ups and downs,
For every challenge is a lesson in disguise.
Be kind to yourself, especially during hard
times,
And trust that you are growing into someone
extraordinary.

Though the path may not always be clear,

Every step you take brings you closer to
becoming who you're meant to be.
Keep moving forward with hope,
And remember, you are more powerful than you
know.

Precious moments

As you grow, my precious daughter,
Every moment feels like a fleeting treasure.
Your small hands, exploring the world with
wonder,
Your laughter, a bright light in our home.

I wish I could pause these days,
To keep you as you are now,
A little star shining with innocence and joy.

Each day you grow and change,
And while I marvel at your growth,
I can't help but wish to hold onto these moments.

The way you look at the world with fresh eyes,
The way your smile lights up the room.

I want to keep you just like this,
A perfect snapshot of childhood,
In a time that seems all too short.

Yet I know that with each new day,
You'll blossom into something more,
And while I'll cherish every stage,
I'll forever hold these precious times close to my
heart.

Perfect fit

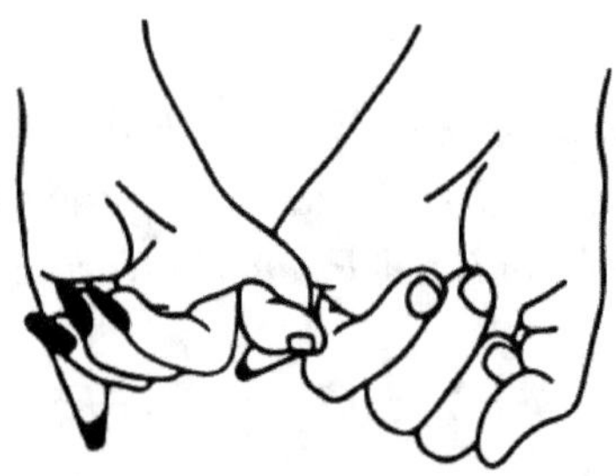

*In the realm of heartache, where past wounds
shape our stories,
Life orchestrates a beautiful meeting of two
souls.*

*Each carrying their own burden of broken
dreams and lost love,
Finding solace in the other's company.
Their paths cross at a time when healing begins,*

*And the fragments of their hearts start to mend
together.
What was once a maze of pain and sorrow,
Now becomes a mosaic of shared understanding
and warmth.*

*In the gentle exchange of glances and the
comfort of shared silence,
They discover a connection that goes beyond the
past.*

A union formed from the pieces of their hearts,
Creating something beautiful and whole from
what was once shattered.

Journey to love

*In the soft glow of shared laughter and quiet
conversations,
Where trust grows deeper with every secret
shared,
A simple friendship begins to evolve.*

*What starts as a connection marked by
understanding,
Slowly transforms into something more
profound.*

*As the bond strengthens, the lines blur,
Between confidant and partner, friend and lover.
Every shared moment of joy and sorrow,
Every whispered word and knowing glance,*

*Builds a foundation of love that feels both
familiar and new.
This love is not sudden, but a gentle unfolding,*

*A natural progression from deep understanding
to a cherished partnership.*

*In each other, you find not only a friend but a
soulmate,*
*The one who completes the story you've been
writing together.*

*From the warmth of friendship to the fire of true
love,*
*You discover a connection that is both tender
and enduring.*

Cosmic Request

Oh stars, glittering in the night sky,
I send this playful plea into the universe,
Hoping you'll find me a partner in crime,
Someone who'll rise at 3 AM just to hear my
ramblings.

I'm looking for a soul who'll dance with wild
joy,
As if the world is their stage and no one is
watching,
Twisting and spinning through the living room
with me.

Let them be the one who'll join me in culinary
chaos,
Mixing ingredients with laughter and a hint of
mischief,
Turning every meal into an adventure.

Grant me this whimsical wish,
A co-adventurer who'll make every day a new
escapade,
Filling our lives with spontaneous joy and
endless fun.

Let our days be a series of delightful, unplanned
moments,
A testament to the magic of life and love.

Letter to my daughter

Dear Future Daughter,
As you venture into the world,
Know that my love is always with you,
Even when we are apart.

Each step you take is a new chapter in your
story,
A journey filled with both joy and challenges.

May you find beauty in the simple moments,
And may kindness be your constant companion.

Let your spirit soar high,
Reaching for the stars with every dream you
chase.

In every experience, I see the reflection of my
hopes,
A future bright with endless possibilities.

I am eager to see the person you become,
As you write your own story,
Filled with courage, grace, and love.

Know that I will always be cheering for you,
Every step of the way.

All my love – Mom

Dance at work

In the maze of ice cubicles, connections form
Not always by choice, but by necessity
Faces become familiar, names are spoken often
Shared work creates bonds, fragile yet real

Moments of collaboration, where ideas merge
And times of tension, where patience is tested
Conversations over coffee and small talk at the
lift lobby
Slowly build a network of understanding and
support

Conflicts arise, and resolutions are negotiated
Trust is earned, sometimes over months or years
Encouragements are given, and feedback is
exchanged
In the rhythm of daily tasks, relationships evolve

We celebrate successes together, and console
through failures

*Each person a thread in the complex fabric of
the workplace
Together, we navigate challenges and victories
Creating a mosaic of human interaction and
shared goals*

The lonely Bench

In an empty park, a bench sits beneath an old oak tree
Its wood is worn and splintered, weathered by time

The paint has faded, and the metal supports are rusted
It faces a quiet view, perhaps of a pond or a garden

The bench waits in solitude, its surface untouched
It has seen many people come and go, some sitting for hours

Lost in thoughts, conversations, or simply enjoying the peace
Now, it sits vacant, holding the echoes of past moments

Around it, the world moves on – children play, birds sing

But the bench remains in its place, a silent witness

It waits for the next visitor, a brief respite from the world
Or perhaps it simply exists, a quiet piece of the landscape

Quiet Library

Rows of bookshelves stretch endlessly in all
directions
Each shelf a repository of knowledge, stories,
and dreams

The air is still, holding the soft scent of paper
and ink
Gentle light filters through tall windows, casting
a calm glow

Patrons move silently between the aisles
Their footsteps are muffled, their whispers
barely audible

The soft rustle of pages turning is the only sound
A place where time seems to slow, where focus
deepens

*In this digital world, I still find solace in
physical books
Their smell, the texture of the paper, and their
rich history*

*A connection to the past, and a reminder of
timeless knowledge
The library is a sanctuary, a haven from the
outside noise*

Women

In a world full of noise and competition
Women come together, offering strength and
support
Encouragement flows freely, shared in words
and actions
A network of solidarity, a community of empathy

They celebrate each other's achievements, big
and small
Lift each other up through challenges and
doubts
Their voices are a chorus of praise and
reassurance
Each act of kindness weaves a stronger bond

Together, they forge paths, overcome barriers
Offering a hand and a listening ear when needed
In their unity, they find empowerment and hope
Women who uplift each other create a powerful
force